MAKING MUSICAL INSTRUMENTS

By Dana Meachen Rau • Illustrated by Kathleen Petelinsek

CHERRY LAKE PUBLISHING • ANN ARBOR, MICHIGAN

CHERRY
LAKE
Publishing

Published in the United States of America by Cherry Lake Publishing
Ann Arbor, Michigan
www.cherrylakepublishing.com

Photo Credits: Page 4, ©TunedIn by Westend61/Shutterstock; page 5, ©val lawless/Shutterstock; page 6, ©Dolly MJ/Shutterstock; page 7, ©IngoSStar/Shutterstock; page 11; ©Charlie Rau; page 22, ©VICTOR TORRES/Shutterstock; page 29, ©SpeedKingz/Shutterstock.

Library of Congress Cataloging-in-Publication Data
Names: Rau, Dana Meachen, 1971– author.
Title: Making musical instruments / by Dana Meachen Rau.
Description: Ann Arbor, Michigan : Cherry Lake Publishing, [2016] |
Series:
   How-to library | Series: Crafts | Includes bibliographical references
   and index.
Identifiers: LCCN 2016000986| ISBN 9781634714211 (lib. bdg.) |
ISBN 9781634714297 (pdf) | ISBN 9781634714372 (pbk.) | ISBN
9781634714457 (ebook)

Subjects: LCSH: Musical instruments—Construction—Juvenile literature.
Classification: LCC ML460 .R323 2016 | DDC 784.192/3—dc23
LC record available at http://lccn.loc.gov/2016000986

Cherry Lake Publishing would like to acknowledge the work of the
Partnership for 21st Century Learning. Please visit www.p21.org
for more information.

Printed in the United States of America
Corporate Graphics
July 2016

HOW-TO LIBRARY

TABLE OF CONTENTS

Making More Than Music

Drums are one of the most common kinds of percussion instruments.

Making music is marvelous. By banging, strumming, and blowing into instruments, you can create sounds that blend together to form a tune. There are four basic types of instruments: percussion, brass, woodwind, and string.

Percussion instruments are the type you hit with your hands or some other object to make a sound. These include drums and xylophones.

Brass instruments are made of metal and need air to work. You blow air into a mouthpiece. This air travels through the instrument and makes sound. Trombones, trumpets, and tubas are types of brass instruments.

Woodwinds also need air to work. You blow air over a small piece of wood called a reed. The reed vibrates and makes a sound. Clarinets and oboes are woodwinds.

String instruments make sounds when you pluck, strum, or slide a bow across their strings. String instruments include guitars, violins, and harps.

You can make a lot of beautiful music with these instruments. But you can also make your own instruments and create your own unique tunes! All it takes are some simple supplies!

Playing many kinds of instruments together can create rich, interesting music.

From the Beginning

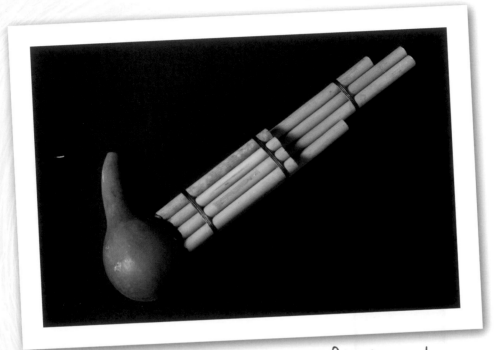

This traditional instrument is made of bamboo and a dried gourd.

Musical instruments have been around for as long as there have been people to play them. Ancient people made the earliest instruments out of stones, bones, shells, animal skins, seeds, and wood. These were items they could find easily in nature.

People played instruments for many reasons. Music was often an important part of a community's **rituals** or a way to worship gods. Other times, musical instruments had a more **practical** use. People might use them to call animals in from a field or to communicate with distant villages.

People around the world developed different instruments and musical styles. Africa was known for its variety of drums. String instruments became very popular in Europe. As people traveled beyond their borders and traded goods, musical ideas traveled with them. This led to the creation of even more types of instruments and musical styles. Other inventions led to new instruments and ideas as well. For example, the discovery of electricity led to instruments such as keyboards and electric guitars.

New kinds of music continue to develop even today. Now it's time for you to create your own musical style. Let's make some instruments!

Keyboards and other electronic instruments cannot make sound unless they are plugged in or using batteries.

Basic Supplies

Musical instruments are made from all sorts of materials. Some traditional instruments, such as washboards and jugs, are made using inexpensive everyday objects. Other instruments, such as Stradivarius violins, are considered priceless works of art. They are made from quality materials by expert builders.

You don't need to buy any expensive supplies to make the instruments in this book. Here are some of the items you will need:

General Supplies:
- Cardboard
- Pencil
- Ruler
- Rubber bands
- Tools for cutting: scissors, fabric scissors, and a craft knife
- **Adhesives**: tacky glue, hot glue gun, masking tape, and duct tape

From Around the House:
- Waxed paper
- Aluminum foil

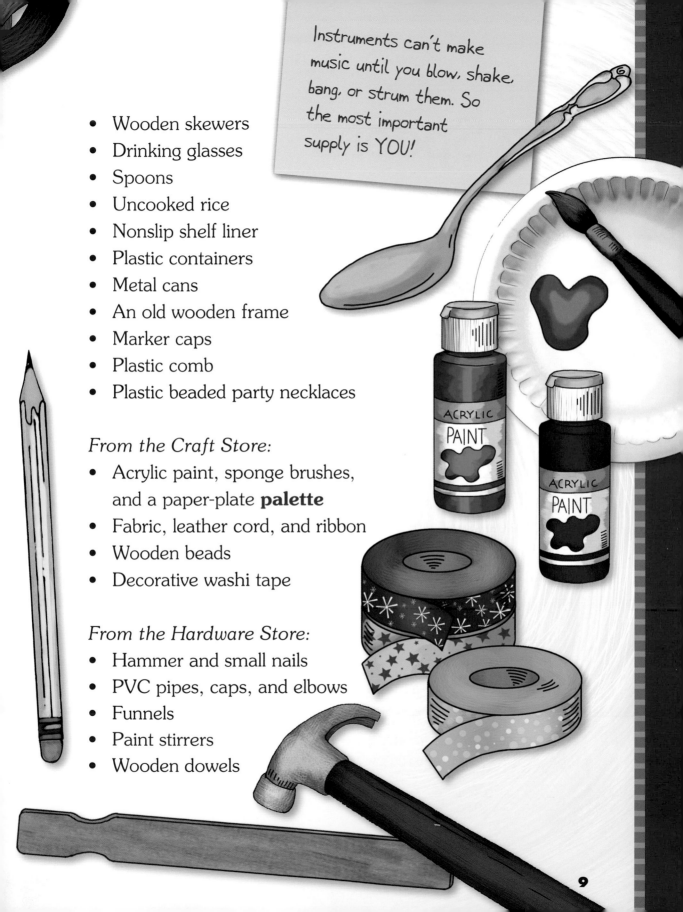

- Wooden skewers
- Drinking glasses
- Spoons
- Uncooked rice
- Nonslip shelf liner
- Plastic containers
- Metal cans
- An old wooden frame
- Marker caps
- Plastic comb
- Plastic beaded party necklaces

From the Craft Store:
- Acrylic paint, sponge brushes, and a paper-plate **palette**
- Fabric, leather cord, and ribbon
- Wooden beads
- Decorative washi tape

From the Hardware Store:
- Hammer and small nails
- PVC pipes, caps, and elbows
- Funnels
- Paint stirrers
- Wooden dowels

Instruments can't make music until you blow, shake, bang, or strum them. So the most important supply is YOU!

The Spoons

To make this instrument, you don't need to build anything at all! All you need are two metal spoons from your kitchen drawer. You can also find inexpensive spoons at discount stores or tag sales.

Materials
- Two metal spoons of the same size
- Your hands
- Your knees

Steps
1. Hold the spoons so their back sides are facing each other. Place your fingers between the spoons' handles so your thumb is on top, your index finger is between the handles, and your middle finger is below. Slide the ends of the handles into your palm and close your fingers around them. You should have a firm grip, and there should be a small space between the bowls of the spoons.

2. Tap the bottom spoon on your knee. You'll hear a clicking sound as the bowls of the spoons hit each other. You don't need to move your fingers. It's the movement of the spoons that makes the sound. Practice making a steady beat of clicks.

3. Hover your other palm above the spoons. They should hit your open hand after bouncing up from your knee. This adds another beat to the rhythm.

4. Try playing in different ways. Speed up, slow down, tap softer, and tap harder. Try playing the spoons on different parts of your leg or up your arm. Experiment with different **rhythms**.

Try playing the spoons in different ways to produce different sounds.

Washboard

Washboards were once used for washing clothing. People soaked their clothing and then rubbed it against the ridges of the board to help scrub out dirt. Washboards were first made from wood. Later, they were made from metal. When people realized that running their fingers along the board's ridges made an interesting sound, it became a percussion instrument!

Materials

- Two pieces of cardboard, cut to 8 by 11 inches (20.3 by 28 centimeters)
- Pencil
- Ruler
- Craft knife and scissors
- Tacky glue
- About 70 6-inch (15.2 cm) wooden skewers
- Heavy books
- 24-inch (61 cm) length of ribbon
- Masking tape
- Marker caps

Steps

1. Measure and draw a 1.5-inch (3.8 cm) frame on each piece of cardboard. Use a craft knife to cut out the inside of the frame on one piece. Set this frame and inside piece aside.

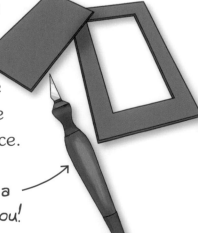

Always get help from an adult when using a craft knife. It is very sharp and can cut you!

2. Glue the skewers across the center area of the frame on the other piece of cardboard. Place them as close together as possible.

3. Cut two strips of cardboard from the inside piece you cut out in step 1. Glue these to the short edges of the piece with the skewers. This will help raise up the sides so that they are level with the skewers.

4. Spread glue around all four edges of the cut-out frame. Place the frame on top of the cardboard and skewers like a sandwich. Be sure all the edges line up. Place the washboard under some heavy books to help press it all together. Let the glue dry completely.

5. Tape the ends of the ribbon to the back of the washboard. When you wear it around your neck, the washboard should sit in the middle of your chest.

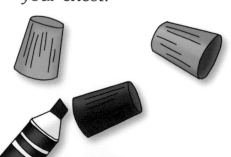

HOW TO PLAY

Place the washboard around your neck and the marker caps on your fingertips. Tap a beat on the washboard. Then run your fingers up and down the ridges of the skewers to make a scraping sound.

13

Waxed Paper Harmonica

Historians believe the earliest harmonica was invented in China thousands of years ago. This instrument was called a sheng. Harmonicas as we know them today were invented in Germany in the 1800s. Musicians play the harmonica by blowing out and sucking in air through its holes. The reeds inside this woodwind instrument vibrate to produce sound. You can create your own harmonica with some simple materials.

Materials
- Waxed paper
- Plastic comb
- Scissors
- Washi tape

Steps
1. Cut a piece of waxed paper to be larger than your comb. Place the comb on the paper, then fold the paper in half so the teeth of the comb are in the fold.

2. Cut off the extra waxed paper along the bottom of the comb. Place a piece of washi tape along this edge. Fold the tape over so the comb is secure inside the sleeve of waxed paper.

3. Trim off the excess waxed paper and tape from the ends of the comb.

HOW TO PLAY

Grip your harmonica at its corners. Hold it up to your lips and make a humming sound against the comb's teeth, then part your lips slightly. The vibrations of the waxed paper will create a buzzing noise.

Rainstick

This South American instrument is usually made by filling dried stalks of cacti with seeds or pebbles. People played it during long periods of dry weather when they hoped for rain.

Materials

- One 24-inch (61 cm) length of 2-inch-wide (5 cm) PVC pipe
- Acrylic paint, sponge brush, and palette
- Aluminum foil
- Scissors
- Two 2-inch-wide (5 cm) PVC cap sockets
- Piece of paper
- ½ cup (118.3 milliliters) of uncooked rice
- Three 24-inch (61 cm) lengths of ribbon

Steps

1. Paint the PVC pipe to look like a stalk of cactus. Set it aside until the paint dries completely.
2. Cut a piece of aluminum foil to be about one and a half times the length of your pipe. Roll it into a

PAINTING TIP

To make cleanup easy, use a paper plate as a palette to hold and mix your paint. You can simply toss it out when you are done.

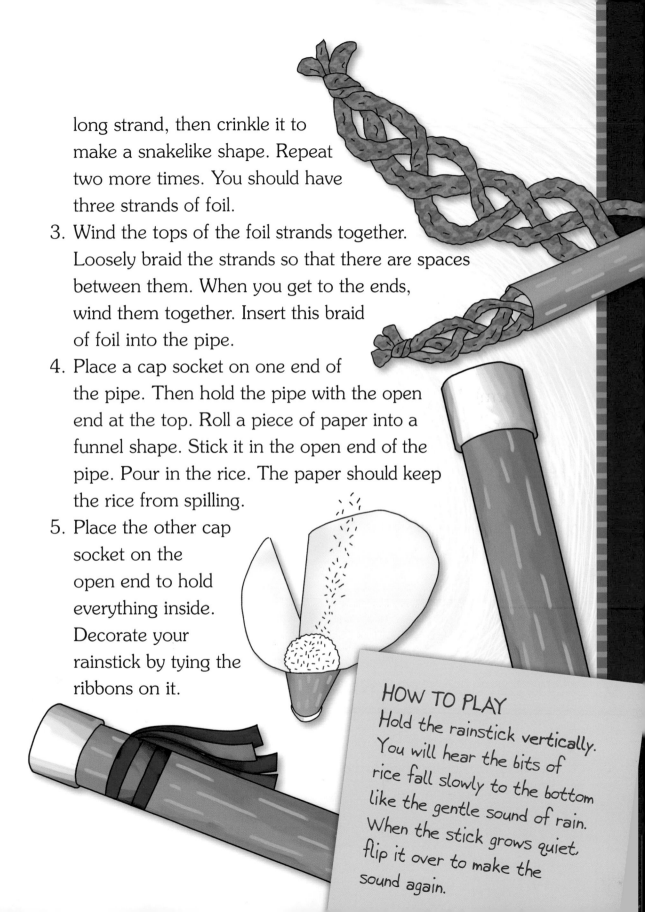

long strand, then crinkle it to make a snakelike shape. Repeat two more times. You should have three strands of foil.

3. Wind the tops of the foil strands together. Loosely braid the strands so that there are spaces between them. When you get to the ends, wind them together. Insert this braid of foil into the pipe.

4. Place a cap socket on one end of the pipe. Then hold the pipe with the open end at the top. Roll a piece of paper into a funnel shape. Stick it in the open end of the pipe. Pour in the rice. The paper should keep the rice from spilling.

5. Place the other cap socket on the open end to hold everything inside. Decorate your rainstick by tying the ribbons on it.

HOW TO PLAY

Hold the rainstick vertically. You will hear the bits of rice fall slowly to the bottom like the gentle sound of rain. When the stick grows quiet, flip it over to make the sound again.

Water Glasses

For hundreds of years, people have made music by gently
tapping glasses of water. This musical marvel began in Persia
and later spread to Europe. By the 18th century, musicians were
writing music and performing concerts using water glasses.

Materials

- Nonslip shelf liner
- Eight drinking glasses of the same size and shape
- Pitcher of water
- Small metal spoon

Steps

1. Place the shelf liner on a table or counter. Line up your glasses on the liner. Pour different levels of water into the glasses. They should range from almost empty to almost full.

2. Tap the spoon very gently on the side of each glass near the top rim. Listen to the sounds you create. Notice how the notes change depending on how much water is in the glass.

3. Play a tune!

An octave is a series of eight notes that form a musical scale. The notes range from low to high.

Rubber Band Harp

Images of harps have been found in ancient Egyptian paintings dating back more than 4,000 years. Today, harps are one of the largest instruments in an **orchestra**. A player sits at a stool and balances the harp on his or her shoulder. The harp you'll be making isn't nearly so large. It can fit in your lap!

Materials
- An old wooden frame, no bigger than 8 by 10 inches (20.3 by 25.4 cm)
- Ruler
- Pencil
- Hammer
- Small nails with large heads, such as upholstery tacks
- Rubber bands in various sizes

Steps
1. Start at a corner of the frame. Measure and mark a dot every 1 inch (2.5 cm) along one of the long sides and one of the short sides.

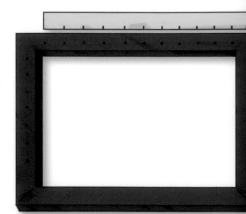

2. Hammer the nails into the dots along the short side. Then hammer an equal number of nails into the dots along the long side. You won't nail into all the dots on the long side.

3. Starting with the smallest rubber bands first, string your harp by stretching a rubber band from the first nail on the short side to the first nail on the long side.

4. Repeat with the second nails, then the third nails, and so on. If the rubber bands get too hard to stretch and cannot reach between the nails, switch to the next size up. Continue until there are bands on all the nails.

HOW TO PLAY
Rest the frame in your lap. The longest bands should be closest to you. The shortest should be farthest away. Gently pluck the bands to make a twanging sound.

Alphorn

Some alphorns are very long!

The alphorn is a long horn made of wood and has been used for hundreds of years in Switzerland. People once played the alphorn to communicate with each other across mountain valleys. Today, musicians play it at festivals to celebrate this tradition. It has become a symbol of Switzerland.

Materials
- Small funnel
- One 60-inch (152.4 cm) length of 1.5-inch-wide (3.8 cm) PVC pipe
- Duct tape
- Large funnel
- One 1.5-inch-wide (3.8 cm) PVC 90-degree sweep elbow

Steps

1. Place the wide end of the small funnel on one end of the pipe and secure it with duct tape. This will be your mouthpiece.

2. Insert the narrow end of the large funnel into one end of the sweep elbow and secure it with duct tape.

3. Secure the sweep elbow onto the open end of the pipe.

HOW TO PLAY

Stand up while holding the long pipe in your hands. Rest the large funnel on the floor. Place your lips together and push air out to make a buzzing noise into the mouthpiece.

Cabasa

Cabasas were invented in Africa. They were originally made of dried **gourds** and beads. They then became popular in Latin music and were made of metal and wood. The sound of the beads rattling against each other and rolling around the central base sounds like the hissing of a rattlesnake.

Materials
- At least six plastic beaded party necklaces
- Large metal coffee can with plastic lid
- Scissors
- Craft knife
- 12-inch (30.5 cm) dowel
- Duct tape
- Hot glue gun

Steps
1. Cut the necklaces to make a bunch of bead strands. Wrap one around the can. Connect the ends by crossing the string between two beads. Twist it around a few times to secure it and trim off the extra beads. You want the loop of beads tight enough to stay on the can but loose enough to roll freely.

2. Repeat with the rest of the strands until the whole can is covered.

3. Use a craft knife to cut two slits in the plastic lid in an X shape. Insert the dowel until it touches the bottom of the can.

4. Take off the lid. Secure the dowel to the inside of the lid with duct tape. Squeeze hot glue into the center of the bottom of the can. Then place the lid back on, making sure that the dowel is touching the glue at the bottom. Let the glue dry completely.

Always get help from an adult when using a craft knife or a hot glue gun. The knife is very sharp, and the glue gun is very hot!

HOW TO PLAY
There are a few ways to play the cabasa. You can shake it like a rattle so the beads hit against the base. You can tap the beads against your open palm. You can also rub your fingers across the beads so they roll around the metal base.

Damaru

A damaru is a two-headed drum. Beads strike the center of each drum to make a *dum*, *dum*, *dum* sound. This drum plays a very important role in the traditions of Hinduism and Buddhism.

Materials

- Two plastic containers
- Thin fabric
- Pencil
- Ruler
- Fabric scissors
- Two rubber bands
- 24-inch (61 cm) length of leather cord
- Two wooden beads
- Hot glue gun
- Wooden paint stirrer

Steps

1. Place one container facedown on the fabric and trace around the edges with a pencil. Then cut out the fabric about 1 inch (2.5 cm) outside your pencil line. Repeat with the other container.

2. Stretch the fabric circles over the tops of the containers and hold them in place with the rubber bands.

3. Tie a knot about 2 inches (5.1 cm) from one end of the cord. Thread a bead onto the cord. Tie another knot to hold it in place.

4. Place the bead in the center of one drum. Fold the cord around to the bottom of the container. Glue it into place.

5. Glue the paint stirrer across the bottom of the container **perpendicular** to the cord.

Always get help from an adult when using a hot glue gun. It is very hot and can burn you!

6. Then glue the bottom of the other container on top of the stirrer. You'll have a sandwich of drums with the stirrer and cord in the middle.

7. Bring around the other end of the cord to the face of the second drum. Tie a knot almost at the center. Thread on a bead, then tie another knot to hold it in place. Trim off the extra cord.

HOW TO PLAY

Hold the handle of the damaru upright so that your thumb is flat on one side of the stirrer and your fingers are on the other side. Turn your wrist slightly back and forth so one drum is facing you, and then the other. Continue making this motion to get the beads moving. They will strike the surface of each drum as you turn your wrist.

The More the Merrier

One of the most important parts of playing a musical instrument is practice. The more you practice, the better you'll get at creating amazing sounds with your instruments. When you feel ready, put on a show for an audience!

You don't have to be a one-person show. Invite a bunch of friends over. Imagine you are working in a music studio. Let everyone try out the instruments, and then form a band. You can even record a song!

It's the more the merrier when it comes to friends— and music!

What kind of music will you make?

Glossary

adhesives (ad-HEE-sivz) substances, such as glue, that make things stick together

gourds (GORDZ) hard-skinned fruits that grow on vines

orchestra (OR-kes-truh) a large group of musicians playing instruments together

palette (PAL-it) a flat board for holding and mixing paints

perpendicular (pur-pen-DIK-yuh-lur) at right angles to another line or surface

practical (PRAK-ti-kuhl) useful and sensible

rhythm (RITH-uhm) a repeated pattern of sound in music

rituals (RICH-oo-uhlz) acts that are always performed in the same way, usually as part of a religious or social ceremony

vertically (VUR-ti-klee) in an up-and-down direction

For More Information

Books

Ardley, Neil. *Music*. New York: DK Publishing, 2004.

Krull, Kathleen. *Lives of the Musicians: Good Times, Bad Times (and What the Neighbors Thought)*. San Diego: Harcourt, 2002.

McDonough, Yona Zeldis. *Who Was Louis Armstrong?* New York: Grosset and Dunlap, 2004.

Wiseman, Ann Sayre, and John Langstaff. *Making Music*. North Adams, MA: Storey Kids, 2003.

Web Sites

New York Philharmonic Kids Zone

www.nyphilkids.org/games/main.phtml

This site is full of games and activities to help you learn more about orchestras.

Yale School of Music: Collection of Musical Instruments

http://collection.yale.edu/

View this online exhibit of beautiful instruments of all kinds.

Index

About the Author

Dana Meachen Rau is the author of more than 300 books for children on many topics, including science, history, cooking, and crafts. She creates, experiments, researches, and writes from her home office in Burlington, Connecticut.